PETER'S VISION

Beacon or Bacon?

A  Book ©

Robin Gould, D.R.E., LMFT

This booklet is a BEKY Book publication:
Books Encouraging the Kingdom of Yeshua.

www.bekybooks.com

DEDICATION

This book is dedicated to my son, Daniel, who always walks in bravery as a beacon of light in a dark world. His courage and strength of heart inspires me. Semper Fi.

Ooh-rah!

CONTENTS

GLOSSARY

Sin - to transgress the law (1 John: 3-4).

Bound - betrothed or separated, but not divorced or married.

Loosed - widowed or divorced.

Colander - a device for sifting; it separates items of different sizes.

Common - regarded as unclean by subjective interpretation or deemed to be actually unclean due to empirical uncleanness as defined by Torah law.

Unclean - deemed unclean by Torah law.

ESL - abbreviation for "English as a Second Language."

Redeemed - mercifully pardoned from wrath justifiably scheduled due to guilt.

Incantation - the chanting or uttering of words purporting to have magical power, the formula employed; a spell or charm.

God-Fearer - a God-fearer is a Gentile, a "proselyte of the gate," who has accepted the one God of Israel and who has begun to keep some of the commandments. For instance, Cornelius the God-fearer observed the Jewish hour of prayer.

Vernacular - the language or dialect spoken by the ordinary people in a particular country or region.

Beacon - a light or other visible object serving as a signal, warning, or guide, especially at sea or on an airfield.

Oral Law - the Jewish oral law traditionally believed to have been passed down from Moses. Yeshua usually upheld the oral law of the House of Hillel, but he overruled most of the oral laws of the House of Shammai. They were the two predominant schools of the Pharisees in the First Century.

Rabbinic law - directives enacted by Jewish scholars which have the force of community law. The authority to enact *takkanot* (rabbinic law) is derived from Deuteronomy 17:11. Also see Oral Law.

Torah - the first five books of the Bible, misunderstood as "law" in English translations. The Torah is more accurately God's teaching and instruction. It contains topics such as science, history, priestly procedures, civil statutes, ordinances, health, agriculture, commandments, prophecies, prayer, animal husbandry, architecture, civics, and many others. The root word of Torah comes from the Hebrew word *yarah*, which means "to hit the mark." Torah may also be used to refer to all of the Hebrew Bible, or even to its smallest meaning, a procedure. Torah may be used by Messianic Jews to refer to the entire Bible from Genesis to Revelation, for the Torah is the foundation for all the Scriptures. The Prophets point Israel back to the Torah. The Psalms teach one to love the Torah as King David loved it. The Writings teach the consequences of departing from the Torah and the rewards for returning to it. The New Testament brings the Torah to its fullest meaning in the person Yeshua the Messiah, and much of the New Testament quotes the Tanakh.

Sanhedrin - an authoritative religious assembly or court in the Land of Israel. Although its powers were increased or limited at various times in Jewish history since the return from Babylon, some responsibilities were: supervising the Temple service, deciding as to the harvest tithes, sitting in civil judgment, arranging the calendar, providing correct copies of the Torah roll for the king, and probably for the Temple, deciding all doubtful questions relating to the religious law and rendering the final decision.

1

HISTORY FOR CONTEXT

Bacon has become one of the most popular menu items of the contemporary food scene. A bacon fan can order up bacon popcorn, bacon chocolate, bacon ice cream, bacon-flavored salt (ironically made without bacon), even a bacon-enhanced apostle of Yeshua![1] From bacon air fresheners to bacon clothing logos, the obsession is clear; bacon, bacon, bacon!

Peter's rooftop vision is a popular proof text used to discourage followers of Messiah Yeshua from obeying the Bible's dietary laws that prohibit certain meats, such as bacon, that God has declared to be unclean. Peter was a zealous figure who, at times, misunderstood Yeshua's evangelistic mission and missed the bigger picture. To improve his spiritual view, Peter was given a weighty intervention in the form of a vision. Many who shake their heads sagely as they read of Peter's mistakes might themselves be misunderstanding Yeshua's mission, partly by misunderstanding Peter's vision. In the end, Peter did interpret his vision correctly, though his words have become lost in a modern narrative that replaces Peter's report of the meaning of his vision. 1. Jesus

This booklet examines Peter's vision in the proper linguistic, historical, and Word-based context for accurate study and understanding. The result is the Good News taking deeper root in our lives.

Peter

Simon Peter was a married man[2] who, along with his brother Andrew, was an apostle of Yeshua. He is noted for his incredible vision of the animals descending in a sheet. In biblical history, Peter is remembered as the Jewish apostle who was commissioned by the Messiah to seek out Gentiles and preach the gospel to them.[3] These are biblical facts.

There are assumptions in the mainstream about Peter that are not facts. For instance, Peter has been attributed by man more than the apostolic authority invested in him by Yeshua. An examination of Peter's authority is vital, for misconceptions have opened the door for erroneous teaching regarding his words and intentions. One misconstruction is that Peter is the first "Pope" corresponding with the Papacy's doctrinal view of such a role/figure, and that all Popes in the history of the Church are successors of Peter, who represented and embraced this unlimited authority. No disrespect to the Catholic Church is intended by this analysis; the goal is to gather and promote factual, verifiable information so we may be well-informed students of the Word of God.

The Pope

To get a sense of the Catholic view of Peter as the original Pope, let's look at how this mantle is viewed in the system which promotes it. The Pope, whose title is derived from the Latin Papa (as in "father"), is the Bishop of Rome, the world leader of the Catholic Church, and head of the Vatican, which is the sovereign city-state within Rome. (Ratzinger, 1994). The role of the Pope is the "unifier" between God and the Church, and he is the inerrant Holy One

2. Matt 8:14

3. Acts 9:32; 10:2

10

(Foley & Coffey, 1923). The Pope can alter biblical doctrine as he sees fit, and he is not to be questioned. His position as an elected figure by Catholic clergy is regarded as an anointed office of unparalleled power. (ibid)

Considered the voice of the Church, for the Church, he stands as the representative of Christ on earth. "We have in the authoritative voice of the Church, the voice of Christ Himself. The Church is above the Bible; and this transference of Sabbath observance from Saturday to Sunday is proof positive of that fact." (ibid).

Generally, Protestant denominations reject the notion that any man is inerrant as well as the notion that the Bible is secondary in terms of authority to the doctrines of the church. The Protestant segment of believers usually sees the Messiah as the unifier and mediator between God and man. This is one of the primary demarcations between Protestant and Catholic doctrines, though there are other differences as well. However, this perception of Peter as divine administrator of ordinances is contradictory to the Bible and is so pervasive that it has permeated and infected even Protestant systems to misconceive Peter's role and message.

Would the real Peter please stand up?

The *Catechism of the Catholic Church* ("The Keys to the Kingdom," #552) declares of Peter, "Because of the faith he confessed, Peter will remain the unshakeable rock of the Church." However, the Bible articulates a different account of Peter. First, there is no biblical record of him referred to as "Pope."

There is a further deviation between the template of the official figurehead of the Pope and Peter that is much more telling, which was Peter's faith. While Peter followed Yeshua, Peter himself was a person who reportedly demonstrated inconsistent faith.

11

He denied the Messiah three times. In fact, Yeshua Himself told Peter he had little faith. "O you of little faith, why did you doubt?"[4]

With no role of the Pope taught anywhere in the Bible, and with Peter, the template figurehead of the Pope *lacking the main attributes the Roman Church asserts as the qualifier* for such a governing office (exceptional, demonstrated faith), there is a large discrepancy. In fact, the Biblical text puts forth Yeshua's brother James as the head of the early Church, not Peter. It was Peter who was called into account for his vision and actions by James and the Jerusalem Council.[5]

What is the premise of this faulty teaching? For every teaching, right or wrong, there is a biblical kernel from which it is grown, with other layers of doctrine piled atop. If the teaching is biblical, things add up consistently, "for precept must be upon precept, line upon line, here a little, there a little."[6] When a concept is not biblically correct at its core, philosophical detours and roundabouts are necessary to make the teaching fit a theological position.

Generally, the unfounded teaching that Peter is the first Pope is the result of the misinterpretation of Matthew's gospel account. "And I tell you, you are Peter, and on this rock I will build my church, and the gates of hell shall not prevail against it."[7] The inaccurate assumption is that Peter is the rock to whom Yeshua refers. Let's look at the actual Greek words used.

What's in a Name?

The name Peter is *Petros* in Greek. It does indeed mean the word "rock"; however, *petros* also means "small stone" or "movable rock." This is a stone one could easily throw or put in his pocket. Yeshua uses this term to refer to Peter. When Yeshua uses the

4. Matt 14:31 NAS

5. Acts 15

6. Isaiah 28:10 KJV

7. Matt 16:18 ESV

word for "rock" *the second time* in that sentence, he does not use the word petros, but instead uses the word *petras,* which means "huge rock," "large cliff," or "immovable rock." These two different words for "rock" are usually translated as one, single word, but Yeshua uses two different terms for a very good reason. The good reason is that they have different meanings. He refers to Peter as Petros (small rock), and He refers to *Himself* as Petras (huge rock).

Yeshua uses both words in the *same sentence* denoting the differences in the terms. In 1 Corinthians 10:4 Paul calls Yeshua the "Rock" *(petras)* as well, so this is not the only time the reference is made. It's understood by the apostles. Being the Messiah, Yeshua is not *a* rock. He is *the* rock. Conversely, Peter, being a follower of the Messiah is not *the* rock. He is *a* rock.

A fuller context of the verses in question is a more scholarly method of answering the question of whether Peter is the rock upon which the Church would be built.

> He said to them, 'But who do
> you say that I am?' Simon Peter
> replied, 'You are the Christ, the
> Son of the living God.' And Jesus
> answered him, 'Blessed are you,
> Simon Bar-Jonah! For flesh and blood
> has not revealed this to you, but
> my Father who is in heaven. And I
> tell you, you are Peter (small rock),
> and on this rock (large rock), I will
> build my church, and the gates of
> hell shall not prevail against it. I will
> give you the keys of the kingdom of
> heaven, and whatever you bind on
> earth shall be bound in heaven, and
> whatever you loose on earth shall be
> loosed in heaven.' Then he strictly
> charged the disciples to tell no one

that he was the Christ." [8]

The conversation leading up to the verse in question is used to reveal the identity of the Messiah as the Anointed One, the One with authority. The identity, of course, is Yeshua. Peter answers this correctly, and Yeshua describes Peter as "blessed" (enviable) for having this knowledge. Yeshua proceeds to clarify that no human, not even Peter, can take credit for this revelation because this was revealed to Peter only by the Father in Heaven. In this declaration, Yeshua is pointing out *the divide* between the Father and Himself as Divine *counterparts* to Peter's human status.

Adonai made humans, and He called them good, so there is nothing wrong with being human as long as we know our place *as humans* and not as Divine figureheads. Yeshua then speaks Peter's name which is a descriptive word for a small, moveable rock. He announces that it is on this "large, immovable rock" (Him) that He will build His church. To paraphrase, "I will build my church (using a little stone, like you, Peter), *on Myself,* the immovable rock, forever."

The foundation of the Church could never be a mere human or a religious system. The foundation is the Messiah, Yeshua. Reading that sentence as if it were about *one rock* rather than *two different rocks* contributes to false assertions:

- The Roman Church replaces the Bible as the final authority.
- Peter is at the head of such an arrangement, the first Pope allegedly elected by the Messiah.

However, reading that sentence as it was actually spoken, highlights Yeshua making clear the lesser role Peter played in comparison with Himself. He chose Peter to be the outreach, yes, but Yeshua makes it clear that He is the immovable rock upon

8. Matt 16:15-20
ESV

which His assembly of Believers would stand. Yes, He would choose and equip Peter to minister *on His behalf*, but not *in place of Him.*

Yeshua assures Peter that He will give him the keys of the kingdom of Heaven as apparatus to carry out this mission, but what Yeshua means by this may be misunderstood. Yeshua narrates this declaration using terms that are adjectives to describe marital status; "bound" and "loosed." These are terms of covenant relating to a bride and her husband.

BOUND: married or betrothed

LOOSED: divorced or widowed

The textual link is to the Bride of Christ and the Bridegroom (Yeshua), and in this context, it explains what these keys will impact. What keys does the Messiah control? Yeshua has control of the ultimate keys of all. "I am he that liveth, and was dead; and, behold, I am alive for evermore, Amen; and have the keys of hell and of death."[9]

This must not be construed to mean that Yeshua was giving Peter authority to make extra-biblical decisions, alter the commandments, or in any way deviate from the Word of Adonai. Rather, He was commissioning Peter *for a purpose*, and affirming that He would provide Peter with the keys to accomplish that commission for His Namesake. Yeshua holds the keys because essentially, *He is the key*. The Messiah's goal is not to bring men into power, but to bring

9. Rev 1:18 KJV

His flock safely into His pasture *by His power.* He will equip those whom He calls with what they need, but power to alter Scripture is not something He has to give, nor would ever consider giving. Yeshua is clear that He Himself did not come to alter even the least of the commandments, so why would He entrust any human being, *let alone* a man of little faith, to do so, for that matter?

> Do not think that I have come to abolish the Law or the Prophets; I have not come to abolish them but to fulfill them. For truly I tell you, until heaven and earth disappear, not the smallest letter, not the least stroke of a pen, will by any means disappear from the Law until everything is accomplished. Therefore anyone who sets aside one of the least of these commands and teaches others accordingly will be called least in the kingdom of heaven, but whoever practices and teaches these commands will be called great in the kingdom of heaven. For I tell you that unless your righteousness surpasses that of the Pharisees and the teachers of the law, you will certainly not enter the kingdom of heaven.[10]

Potato/Potahto Tomato/Tomahto

When a student digs into the Bible to understand the First Century writings from an Ancient Near Eastern, Torah-based perspective, there can be more than one interpretation as to what is being taught. As long as these theories don't violate Torah truth already revealed, it is a matter of interesting study with no harm, no foul. Scholars do not always agree, but if these matters of discussion do not attempt to alter anything established by the Word of truth, then it

10. Matt 5:17-20 KJV

16

can be a matter of speculation that does not cause division and arguments.

This path of tolerance is not often experienced in Western systems of religion, as, frequently, even inconsequential doctrinal beliefs can be an area of denominational territorialism. In Western systems, one group will stand firm on a view of even a small point, and thus require an entirely different building and title from the group on the same street with a different belief on that small point. When you consider the expense and upkeep of a church building that is half full, and then you realize that the same scenario exists in the half full building down the street, unity could be a wonderful answer. Unity is not necessarily conformity, and on these smaller points, unity could improve the capacity of ministry to the poor, for example.

Two different theories of what was meant by "binding and loosing" both bring you to the same conclusion, and this gives an example of how the technicalities of these small matters can be debated safely with no ill effects on the message that the Messiah was conveying. He was always upholding the Torah, proclaiming justice, and looking for His lost sheep. Anything that competes with that is wrong. Anything that agrees with the Messiah's cause, and reasonably accounts for the context and cultural aspects of the period, is fair game. Let's consider two theories.

THEORY #1 Peter: The Colander of the Bride of Christ

Yeshua uses the ancient marriage terminology of "binding" and "loosing" to explain that acceptance or rejection of the terms of the covenant results in marital binding or loosing.

> If he refuses to listen to them, tell it to
> the church; and if he refuses to listen
> even to the church, <u>let him be to you</u>

<u>as a Gentile and a tax collector</u>. Truly I say to you, whatever you bind on earth shall have been bound in heaven; and whatever you loose on earth shall have been loosed in heaven.[11]

In essence, if one rejects the covenant terms, then he or she rejects the covenant benefits and inclusion as the Bride of Adonai.[12] This theory suggests that the "binding and loosing" terminology, which is most often used as a description of marital actions, defines Yeshua's words as a directive to Peter. Peter is given a mission to go out and find the lost sheep from a bridegroom perspective. Yeshua says, "I was sent only for the lost sheep of the house of Israel,"[13] so it is reasonable that He was sending His charge out to sift through the sheep, the true Bride, who would know their True Shepherd.

THEORY #2 Peter: Large and in Charge *or* Small but Called?

Another interpretation regarding this conversation between Yeshua and Peter comes from the historical standpoint that the Pharisees considered themselves as having the authority to "bind" (forbid) and "loose" (permit), behavioral interpretations of the Torah communities that supplanted the commandments over their students, and that Peter was to correct this. Yeshua was quite vocal in many instances of how He hated that some religious leaders of His generation enforced traditions that overrode the actual commandments. Thus, we can reasonably apply the covenantal uses of the words "bind" and "loose" in the context of obedience to the covenant in Matthew's account.

The "keys" are to prevent the second death (spiritual death) which implies safe covenantal status of those to whom Yeshua speaks more than the human leadership upon which the argument focuses. We

11. Matt 18:17-18 ESV

12. Whether this is "written in" or "blotted out" is beyond the topical scope of this booklet.

13. Matt 15:24 ESV

18

must remember, however, that this was not meant by the Messiah to plant an anti-tradition bias. This bias is the common default viewpoint of those not privy to the purpose and utility of oral law traditions, etc., and who have been taught that all oral law was superfluous, extraneous, and to be rejected.[14]

When put into the context that Peter followed the Torah and shared it with the Gentiles so they would be grafted into covenant through the Messiah, the power of binding and loosing could mean that Peter's judgment authority on obvious matters of covenant obedience was being publically affirmed. By declaring Peter's authority, Messiah ensured a way that unity could prevail and make it less complicated to stand together on that Big Rock.

Peter's Torah-informed decisions were to be respected, for the parameters were already established in Heaven by Torah, the Divine Holy Book of Yahweh. Either way, Peter was not instituted as a Pope, nor was he given any authority *above* the Torah, but rather *within* it. (Creeger, S., 2016).[15]

Did you find exploring two different theories interesting? Either of those scenarios are reasonable suggestions. Neither violates Scripture; neither exalts Peter above the Word nor diminishes the importance of his role; and neither requires verse plucking to lend validity. The Word of God is never challenged, "dispensations of time" are not invented, and both are within a scholarly context. "Do your best to present yourself to God as one approved, a worker who has no need to be ashamed, rightly handling the word of truth."[16]

Scripture shows Peter as a follower of Yeshua designated as an authority of judgment within the Torah, which he revered with his whole heart. This is a clear distinction from a religious leader permitted to change the Torah laws, as he is presented in Roman Church perspective.

14. See BEKY Book *Truth, Tradition, or Tare: Growing in the Word* for a full discussion of tradition relative to the truth of the written Word.

15. See *Introduction to the Jewish Sources: Preserving History, Structure, and Heart* by Creeger, S. for further information on traditions and culture from the Messiah's perspective.

16. 2 Tim 2:15 ESV

2

PETER'S VISION OF THE GENTILES

With a better understanding of Peter's role, let's examine his famous vision and determine whether it was a mandate to eat bacon or an admonition against shunning those of other nations from grafting into His one and only Holy nation. The question alone answers itself, but further study yields an important message.

> On the morrow, as they went on their
> journey, and drew nigh unto the city,
> Peter went up upon the housetop
> to pray about the sixth hour: and
> he became very hungry, and would
> have eaten: but while they made
> ready, he fell into a trance, and
> saw heaven opened, and a certain
> vessel descending unto him, as it
> had been a great sheet knit at the
> four corners, and let down to the
> earth: wherein were all manner of
> fourfooted beasts of the earth, and

wild beasts, and creeping things,
and fowls of the air. And there came
a voice to him, 'Rise, Peter; kill, and
eat.' But Peter said, 'Not so, Lord;
for I have never eaten anything
that is common (*koinos*) or unclean
(*akatharton*).' And the voice
spake unto him again the second
time, 'What God hath cleansed,
that call not thou common
(*koinon*).' This was done thrice: and
the vessel was received up again
into heaven. (Acts 10:9-16 KJV)

Q. What was in the sheet?
A: "All kinds of animals and reptiles and birds of the air."

Q: Would some of these animals in the sheet be permissible according to the dietary laws for Peter to "kill and eat?"
A: Yes, because ALL KINDS of animals were in the sheet, both clean and unclean.[17]

We might believe that Peter saw a big sheet full of just pigs, or only unclean animals coming down; however, that was not the case. The Bible reports that all kinds of animals were presented, so *there were clean, Biblically-permitted animals in the sheet.*

The question is, why didn't Peter just kill and eat an animal that was established in the Bible by God as clean for food? Let's put ourselves in Peter's sandals. If you were presented with a barnyard that contained chickens and poisonous blue frogs, and you were instructed: "go, kill and eat," what would you kill and eat? You would kill and eat the animal that you knew was good. You would kill the chicken and eat that without any theological question as to what you were expected to do. Peter could have said, "Okay, I will kill and eat the lamb, cow, chicken, or goat. Thank you, for I am hungry." Our

17. See
Appendix A
for examples
of clean
and unclean
creatures.

22

next question is why didn't Peter do that? Peter did not consider *any* animal in the sheet to be clean... even the animals classified in the Torah as clean.

The reason for this is that Peter and Adonai saw things differently (hence the need for a threefold vision). Peter was not looking at the clean status of the animals in the sheet from a Torah perspective. He saw the animals in the sheet from the viewpoint of the rabbinic additions that were put in place as "fences" to prevent Jews from breaking the actual commandments. The Torah is the Word of Adonai. The rabbinic instructions are the word of man.[18] Yeshua does not honor instructions that replace the Torah commandments or prevent a person from honoring the written Torah, ever.

Peter's vision takes place after Messiah had already come and gone. This was decades later. Here it was, the First Century, and all believers in Messiah observed the Torah, including the dietary laws. The closer to Messiah's physical presence on the Earth, the more Torah-observant His followers were, while subsequent generations became less Torah observant. Even though there were clean animals in the vision, Peter just could not understand how anything in that sheet could be edible. Let's examine Peter's words of protest when told to "go, kill, and eat."

> No, Lord; for I have never eaten anything that is common [*koinon*] or unclean [*akatharton*]. (vs 14 KJV)

What was the response given to Peter's protest?

> And the voice came to him again a second time, 'What God has cleansed, you must not call common [*koinon*]. (vs 15 KJV)

Take a closer look at the two adjectives Peter uses to describe the animals in the sheet. He calls them

18. In her BEKY Book *Introduction to the Jewish Sources* on page 21, Creeger, S. does an excellent job of explaining why the fences were introduced to protect the Word of the Torah; because some commandments carried the death penalty, corporal punishment, or excision from the community, Jewish law added prohibitions designed to make it harder to break the actual Word of God; so many protective fences were added, however, that they sometimes became counter-productive.

"common" (akatharton) and "unclean" (koinon).

It's All Greek to Me.

The Torah has only two classifications for animals: clean or unclean. The identifying characteristics of clean animals are clearly described in Leviticus 11, so the average person is able to obey these commandments easily. The rabbinic additions, however, added a category of unclean for animals that is found nowhere in the Torah. These two classifications are as follows:

1. Things God defined as unclean per their physical characteristics identified in the Word, Leviticus 11.

AND

2. The rabbinic tradition classification of "common," which is a secondary, manmade category of unclean.

"Unclean" in Greek is akatharton. Unclean animals are in this category because the Creator declares it so. This word always means unclean, and in the New Testament, it is usually used to describe unclean spirits. This classification for animals is in the Torah.

"Common" [koinon/koine] in Greek is something "regarded as unclean;" In this meaning it is not sacred or is defiled according to man's standards by touching this item, and therefore become ritually unclean by association. Remember, man declares this so. This word can mean genuinely unclean or only subjectively regarded as unclean, yet not technically unclean per Torah law. This was a familiar label of the First Century in other contexts, but it is not taught in the Torah about animals.

Context, Context, Context!

This does not suggest that the term "common" to

denote unclean was never used by Messiah Yeshua. He did use this word, for it was the vernacular of the day, though of course never when describing animals. Since it did mean "regarded as unclean," it can be interpreted to be genuinely unclean by the Word of God, or merely regarded as unclean by opinion. When used by itself and not in conjunction with the actual word for unclean, it is more likely to be describing something legitimately unclean. Although First Century Greek can be tough for the layperson, examples make the challenge of the language barrier easier to understand.

Imagine explaining to a person learning English that in American culture, we might refer to a woman as a "city girl." That could mean that she actually lives in the city, or it could refer to a woman living in a rural setting who feels more comfortable in an urban environment. The tutor explains that it depends on the context in which the term is used.

EXAMPLE 1

> "Amy lives in small town Mississippi,
> but she is a city girl for sure."

In Example 1, Amy is described as a city girl, though she is not technically a city girl. People familiar with the term "city girl" as a personality description rather than a place of residence will understand the statement, but it is not apparent to someone who learns English as a second language; it must be explained in context.

EXAMPLE 2

> "Amy is a city girl, accustomed to
> living without a car like most of her
> Manhattan neighbors do."

Example 2 is a description of actual residence. This makes more sense to the English-as-a-second-language reader. "City girl" could mean a girl that actually lives in a city *or* it could mean a girl regarded as one who favors the city.

EXAMPLE 3

> "Amy and Cathy are both city girls.
> Amy lives in small town Mississippi,
> but when she visits Cathy in NYC,
> they paint the town red."

In Example 3, the reader would have to know that "small town Mississippi" can mean any small town in Mississippi or any other Southern state. To further complicate matters, ancient Greek, like Hebrew, did not have capital letters or punctuation, so the reader might interpret that Amy lives in a place named Smalltown, Mississippi! After clarifying that, the English tutor would have to convey to our ESL student that NYC stands for New York City, and the idiom of "painting the town red" means to go out and have lots of fun with friends, not to literally start painting the buildings and streets with red paint.

The little ESL exercise demonstrates why it is easy to miss the crucial difference between common and unclean in Peter's response to the command to kill and eat. Understanding the context is always vital in interpreting *koinon* properly since its use was varied, just as some words are in modern English. Whenever a passage in the New Testament appears to contradict a Torah law, press on to see what *you* have missed in translation or context, not what the Torah got wrong. There is always an explanation that proves the Torah to be true and unflawed. When in doubt, reread even a small portion of Psalm 119 or Yeshua's words in Matthew 5, and it resets a straight thinking path.

The words for "common" and "unclean" in our text are used together. In this grammatical context, they are to be regarded in their difference, not in their similarity. Since "common" did mean "regarded as unclean" it can be interpreted, when used by itself, to communicate that the item is genuinely unclean. In this sentence, however, it is used with the actual word for "unclean," thus it does not mean intrinsically unclean here, but unclean by contact or association.

This teaches a valuable lesson about distinctions between man's opinion and God's actual commandments. Did Adonai say anything about the genuinely unclean animals? No. He only spoke of what Peter considered common by association or contact, *koinon*, for, again, there is no category of "common" in the Torah for animals.

Peter walked with the Messiah personally. He may have been a man of little faith in some cases, but he was one of Yeshua's chosen, and he was oriented to His cause. He traveled with Yeshua. He ate with Him. He learned from Him sitting at His feet and hanging on every word He spoke. Years later, still Peter obeys the dietary commandments, but his observance extended beyond what Yeshua taught or what he learned throughout his childhood in Torah study. Peter only saw animals that were unfit for human consumption in the sheet, yet if Adonai was instructing him to "kill and eat," then clearly He presented something in the sheet that would be permissible for Peter to eat. Adonai never breaks His own laws,[19] nor would He tell His children to break them.

19. For an in-depth examination of "Law" and "Torah," see BEKY Book, *What is the Torah?* by H. Alewine.

3

THE GENTILE'S VISION OF PETER

During the time that Peter had his vision of Gentile inclusion with Jewish believers, a Gentile called Cornelius experienced his own vision. Cornelius was stationed in Caesarea, and he was a God-fearing Roman soldier.

> At Caesarea there was a man named Cornelius, a centurion of what was known as the Italian Cohort, a devout man who feared God with all his household, gave alms generously to the people, and prayed continually to God. About the ninth hour of the day he saw clearly in a vision an angel of God come in and say to him, 'Cornelius.' And he stared at him in terror and said, 'What is it, Lord?' And he said to him, 'Your prayers and your alms have ascended as a memorial before God. And now send men to Joppa and bring one Simon who is called Peter. He is lodging with one Simon, a tanner,

whose house is by the sea.' When the angel who spoke to him had departed, he called two of his servants and a devout soldier from among those who attended him, and having related everything to them, he sent them to Joppa.[20]

Peter went with the men, fulfilling his mission as instructed by Yeshua when Yeshua called him the little rock who would bring the sheep to the Big Rock.

And while Peter was pondering the vision, the Spirit said to him, 'Behold, three men are looking for you. Rise and go down and accompany them without hesitation, for I have sent them.' And Peter went down to the men and said, 'I am the one you are looking for. What is the reason for your coming?' And they said, 'Cornelius, a centurion, an upright and God-fearing man, who is well spoken of by the whole Jewish nation, was directed by a holy angel to send for you to come to his house and to hear what you have to say.' So he invited them in to be his guests. The next day he rose and went away with them, and some of the brothers from Joppa accompanied him. And on the following day they entered Caesarea. Cornelius was expecting them and had called together his relatives and close friends. When Peter entered, Cornelius met him and fell down at his feet and worshiped him. But Peter lifted him up, saying, 'Stand up; I too am a man.'[21]

20. Acts 10:1-8 ESV

21. Acts 10:19-26 ESV

30

Peter says that God showed him that he was to go out and find the redeemed, as this was the purpose of the Messiah:

> So Peter opened his mouth and said: 'Truly I understand that God shows no partiality, but in every nation anyone who fears him and does what is right is acceptable to him. As for the word that he sent to Israel, preaching good news of peace through Jesus Christ (he is Lord of all), you yourselves know what happened throughout all Judea, beginning from Galilee after the baptism that John proclaimed: how God anointed Jesus of Nazareth with the Holy Spirit and with power. He went about doing good and healing all who were oppressed by the devil, for God was with him. And we are witnesses of all that he did both in the country of the Jews and in Jerusalem. They put him to death by hanging him on a tree, but God raised him on the third day and made him to appear, not to all the people but to us who had been chosen by God as witnesses, who ate and drank with him after he rose from the dead. And he commanded us to preach to the people and to testify that he is the one appointed by God to be judge of the living and the dead. To him all the prophets bear witness that everyone who believes in him receives forgiveness of sins through his name.' (Acts 10: 34-42 ESV)

The dilemma that Peter faced in his vision of the animals was that Peter considered the clean animals to have been rendered profane (*koinon* - ritually unclean by contact) by being close to the unclean animals that were on the sheet with them. He considered common to be unclean per the rabbinic fence against eating with a Gentile, a fence designed to prevent a Jew from even coming close to foods offered to idols, for it was common practice for meat in the markets to be offered first to idols and for pagan incantations to be made over wine before sale. Only purchases from Jewish vendors could ensure a kosher meat slaughter as commanded in the Torah or that no incantation to another god had been made over the wine.

Yeshua was not against all traditions, just the ones that overrode the commandments or the purpose of the commandments. Peter's thinking was based on rabbinic additions. He had embraced these additions and considered them appropriate. This required correction, as in this case they were overreaching and erroneous, for it prevented a Jew from eating with a God-fearing Gentile.

Adonai was conveying a change in imperative to Peter, for Peter was the one commissioned to go out and be the little rock upon which the One True Rock would build His church. This imperative was a change in which Jewish believers would embrace converts to the faith. Indeed, the Jerusalem Council affirms Peter's interpretation of the vision by imposing two mandates upon the new Gentile believers:

> ...that you abstain from **things sacrificed to idols** and from blood and from **things strangled** and from fornication; if you keep yourselves free from such things, <u>you will do well</u>.[22]

The Greek word for "strangled" *pniktos* is explained in *Harper's Bible Dictionary* as things not slaughtered according to the Jewish rabbinic method. Jews do

22. Acts 15:29

not slaughter unclean animals for consumption. The Jerusalem Council accepts Peter's explanation of his vision as an imperative to open table fellowship to Gentile converts according to the heart of the Torah, which was to embrace people from all nations who wanted to walk in His ways. The vision happened three times.

Peter was equipped to minister to those to whom he was sent, no matter their language, as this was his charge. Cornelius' household embraces Peter's message:

> While Peter was still saying these things, the Holy Spirit fell on all who heard the word. And the believers from among the circumcised who had come with Peter were amazed, because the gift of the Holy Spirit was poured out even on the Gentiles. For they were hearing them speaking in tongues and extolling God. Then Peter declared, 'Can anyone withhold water for baptizing these people, who have received the Holy Spirit just as we have?' And he commanded them to be baptized in the name of Jesus Christ. Then they asked him to remain for some days. (Acts 10, verses 44-48)

Although in Acts Two the Holy Spirit fell on the disciples and they immersed converts (proselytes) to Judaism from every nation, tribe, and tongue, the event at Cornelius' home was the first notable occasion of its kind occurring among the Gentiles who had not yet converted, the "God-fearers." They worshipped the God of Israel and learned the Torah, but they had not yet taken on all the commandments, notably circumcision. The result caused Peter to truly understand the magnitude of this vision. The little rock understood the calling of the Big Rock!

Peter considered the clean animals to have been rendered profane ("ritually unclean") by being close to the unclean animals that were on the sheet near them. Thus, he considered common to be unclean per the rabbinic addition. Again, Yeshua was not against all traditions, just the ones that overrode the commandments or the purpose of the commandments. Peter's thinking was based on a rabbinic addition. He had embraced this addition and considered it appropriate. This required correction, as in this case it prevented fellowship with Gentile believers. Adonai was correcting Peter's thinking by revealing His heart for the nations, as Peter was the one commissioned to go out and be the little rock upon which the One True Rock would build His church. The vision happened three times.

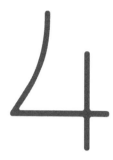

PETER'S INTERPRETATION

Was Peter's vision focused on a new menu for disciples of Yeshua, or was it a turning point in how Jewish believers embraced the God-fearing people among the nations? Peter says that he was shown that Messiah Yeshua was the door for everyone who wanted to walk through it...regardless of DNA.

> And he said to them, 'You yourselves know how unlawful it is for a Jew to associate with or to visit anyone of another nation, but God has shown me that I should not call any **person** common or unclean.' [23]

Peter didn't beckon people to his own "divine" knowledge and opinions. Quite the contrary! He described how God corrected his faulty thinking. That is a far cry from Peter being the first inerrant "Pope" who could administer extra-biblical protocol as an authority. Peter declares that his extra-biblical thinking was corrected!

According to Peter, his vision was not a message about the status of animals. The vision was a message 23. Acts 10:28

about the status of **people**. Peter's words bring up another point that further confuses the matter. Peter seems to be saying that no man can be called unclean. "God has shown me that I should not call any **person** common or unclean." Undoubtedly there are unclean men, so what did Peter mean?

Adonai said, "You shall not call what I have cleansed *common*." Adonai didn't mention the word *unclean*. Peter used an additional word beyond that which God uses to describe what was cleansed, as this was the customary vernacular of his audience. Peter was using the words "common" and "unclean" interchangeably like his audience often did.

While these two words did and do have distinctly different meanings depending on context, Peter is like we are today, explaining what the people needed to know in a manner *they* would understand *then*, not what *we* would understand *now*. Peter explained that he had learned that he was not to consider a man locked permanently in an "outsider status," symbolized as "unclean" like an animal. Adonai cleanses people who repent so they may enter into His covenant. As people who want to be in covenant with the God of Abraham, Isaac, and Jacob, what a relief it is to gain clarity and context for these passages!

Does the Law Isolate or Insulate?

Peter's words in verse 28 also require examination. Peter says it was "unlawful" for a Hebrew man to keep company with a Gentile. Is this where the Torah needs an update? Is this one of the things the Messiah did? Did He correct or update the Torah to alter practice? For those unfamiliar with the differences between Torah law, the oral law, and the rabbinic additions, this could be confusing. These levels of ordinances are three distinct things, but often they are morphed into one by those unfamiliar with what each of these codes of conduct is and from where they originate.

Most have heard that there are several words for "love" in Greek, each meaning a different type of love. Similarly, the word "unlawful" Peter is using in context also has specific applications. Peter used the word *athemiton* for unlawful. *Athémitos* is an adjective derived from "not" and *themis*," denoting a custom which is commonly accepted. *Athémitos* refers to an action acceptable based on the prevailing custom or everyday practice; it is not always founded on the Torah law itself. This word is used only in Acts 10:28; 1 Peter 4:3, and 2 Peter 3:17.

Contrast that word with the word *anomia*, meaning "without Torah law." Just like the word "common" can mean two different things depending on the context, the word *athemetos* is similar. It can mean genuinely unlawful, or it can mean outside of the prevailing custom. "Prevailing custom" does not necessarily imply it is acceptable by Adonai, just that it is a prevalent behavior among the people. Peter uses this word in his letters. Context is established if one usage of it contradicts the Torah, and the other usage of it doesn't. We choose the usage that doesn't contradict.

Peter's audience inherently understood that Torah was not to be challenged. There was no suspicion that Peter would ever suggest abandoning or adjusting any Torah laws. That is a dispute that we wrestle with today, but it was not even a consideration in the understanding of those writing these letters and recording these accounts.

In context with what Peter is saying, the best clue is that nowhere in the Torah is it unlawful for a man to keep company with a non-Jew. Therefore, it is obvious that the context of this word is referring to the custom of the people and not the commandments of God. Here is where the rabbinic opinion contradicted the written law and the proper oral law. It also contradicts the words of the prophets.

> I am the LORD, I have called you
> in righteousness, I will also hold you
> by the hand and watch over you,
> and I will appoint you as a covenant
> to the people, as a light to the
> nations.[24]

The whole purpose of Israel was to demonstrate the blessings of the Law to the Nations. They were commissioned to be a **light to the nations.**

> See, I have taught you decrees
> and laws as the Lord my God
> commanded me, so that you
> may follow them in the land you
> are entering to take possession
> of it. Observe them carefully, for
> this will show your wisdom and
> understanding to the nations, who
> will hear about all these decrees and
> say, 'Surely this great nation is a wise
> and understanding people.' What
> other nation is so great as to have
> their Gods near them the way the
> Lord our God is near us whenever
> we pray to him? And what other
> nation is so great as to have such
> righteous decrees and laws as this
> body of laws I am setting before you
> today? Only be careful, and watch
> yourselves closely so that you do
> not forget the things your eyes have
> seen or let them slip from your heart
> as long as you live. Teach them to
> your children and to their children
> after them.[25]

24. Isaiah 42:6
NAS

25. Deut. 4:5-9
NIV

Peter is discussing the overreaching customs of men. Peter was not explaining that the Law forbade fellowship with Ruth or any other Gentiles who were seeking truth, nor that Yeshua came and did away with that Law. Adonai says that His goal for Israel being given the Torah is to *draw people to it* so they would *want* to join His nation. As you can see, Adonai is proud of His law!

Without knowing the difference between the rabbinic law of that day and the Torah Law, you might assume that Peter was declaring that Adonai was improving or changing His commandments. Rather, what He was doing was correcting Peter for practicing a manmade custom of segregation that prevented the Torah commandments from being a light unto the nations who admired the righteous laws (Torah) of Israel.

If one thought that Peter had the authority to alter commandments, and he thought that Elohim found fault with His own Law[26], he could walk away with a flawed understanding of the steadfastness of the written Word, as well as the limits of Peter as a human being. These misunderstandings have contributed to many unfounded doctrines.

When a society obeys His Law, that society becomes the best example of true love, justice, harmony, and hope. Many view those who love His Torah as losers in bondage, unenlightened, and trying to earn their salvation because they have been taught to view them this way. Here we see the Heavenly Father fighting against man's doctrines and laws to rescue His sheep from another fold. His plan is perfect, but His people are not. Elohim wants us to obey His laws, not to make up our own. His laws bring the sheep home.

Elohim is gathering the Gentiles to Himself to include them with His set-apart, holy people, so would His method be to direct the faithful people to regress to the practices of the Gentiles and eat unclean animals with them, or would He instruct His people to welcome the Gentiles into being a set-apart,

26. For finding fault with **them**, he saith, 'Behold, the days come, saith the Lord, when I will make a new covenant with the house of Israel and with the house of Judah...' (Hebrews 8:8 KJV) The fault was not with the covenant of Torah, but with the people whose hearts were not transformed.

holy people with them? Did Peter say that Adonai told him not to call any **animal** unclean?

No.

So why would we?

Yeshua did not die so that pigs could be made clean; this vision wasn't about animals at all. This vision was about people. Yeshua died so that man could be clean.

At that time Peter and some other believing Jews still observed the rabbinic rule of avoiding being near all non-Jews; this fence ensured they would never violate the commandment that a clean people were to eat clean foods never offered to a pagan god. When the Gentiles began coming to faith, Peter needed to instruct Jewish believers that if Gentiles were believers and lovers of the God of Israel, His Torah, and His People, then they would not contaminate those who walked in the Light of the Word. They also were clean by their living faith that was leading to works.

Faced with a new situation, the Jews considered these believers "common." This was probably justified in the sense that there was hostility toward Jews in most Gentile communities, and many of these new believers still lived in these anti-Semitic Gentile populations. If Peter's calling was to be the little rock who would lead others to the Big Rock, that could not be accomplished with Peter remaining on his own roof. He had to go out and find His sheep, as they would hear the gospel message of their Shepherd and respond.

Yeshua's blood cleanses all mankind who will trust in Him. Adonai told Peter to cease calling common what He had cleansed in spite of his practice of segregation. Yeshua had hinted to it when He cleansed the Temple of the moneychangers who fleeced the Gentiles of their offerings, teaching them that His Father's House was to be called a house of prayer for all nations.[27] Peter's vision firmly embedded Yeshua's message of inclusion, for Peter was commissioned, just as all Israel, as a beacon to the nations. He was an ambassador of the Torah laws, for they bring liberty and protection. Based on factual examination of Peter's words, do you think Adonai was telling Peter that he can feel free to:

a. Break the commandments and eat bacon?

or

b. Go out and preach the gospel to all mankind?

27. Mark 11:17

5

THE SHEET

There is significance to the "certain vessel," usually translated as a sheet, used to present the animals for Peter's consumption.

> And saw heaven opened, and a
> certain vessel descending unto him,
> as it had been a great sheet knit at
> . the four corners, and let down to
> the earth.[28]

This the *tallit gadol,* which is the prayer shawl that Israel uses for prayer to the Most High God. The symbolism is that those represented in the sheet were those who had grabbed onto the fringes (*tzitzit*), and they were grafted into Israel. Tzitzit are associated with people, not animals. A tallit would never be placed on an animal.

Peter, who only saw the outward appearance of a man, was flawed in his perception of who belonged in His flock. All men could become clean, which was the purpose of spreading the new information that the Messiah came for the lost sheep of the house of Israel even if they had been born outside of a tribe of Israel.

28. Acts 10:11 KJV

> **The Heavenly Father was not correcting Peter for obeying His word.**

God's Word said to be a light to the nations because He would be bringing His lost sheep home from all over the planet, and that in God's eyes, the grafted-in are viewed as the same as the native born. The traditional segregation custom that protected Jews kept away the Gentile God-fearers. For disciples of Yeshua, the man-made protection would have to be sacrificed to the weightier matters of justice, mercy, and faithfulness in the Torah, which compelled drawing all men with the same salvation potential, and to bring in the sheep.

What were the acts of the men from Cornelius who also received a vision at that same time? What did they do? The men coming from Joppa did not invite Peter to share a bacon sandwich so that Peter could be converted to the ways of the Gentiles. The men came to Peter for the purpose of learning about Adonai's ways to be set apart.

Could the dream be about people AND animals at the same time?

This is a common suggestion. Some people will go to great lengths to hold on to that bacon! Peter never says that there was a dual purpose to this vision... particularly not one which alters a commandment of Adonai.

A similar confusion is attached to "The Transfiguration." To bolster this point, let's look at another vision for comparison.

> And after six days Jesus took with
> him Peter and James, and John his
> brother, and led them up a high
> mountain by themselves. And he
> was transfigured before them, and
> his face shone like the sun, and
> his clothes became white as light.
> And behold, there appeared to
> them Moses and Elijah, talking with
> him. And Peter said to Jesus, 'Lord,
> it is good that we are here. If you
> wish, I will make three tents here,
> one for you and one for Moses
> and one for Elijah.' He was still
> speaking when, behold, a bright
> cloud overshadowed them, and a
> voice from the cloud said, 'This is my
> beloved Son, with whom I am well
> pleased; listen to him.' When the
> disciples heard this, they fell on their
> faces and were terrified. But Jesus
> came and touched them, saying,
> 'Rise, and have no fear.' And when
> they lifted up their eyes, they saw
> no one but Jesus only. And as they
> were coming down the mountain,
> Jesus commanded them, 'Tell no
> one the vision, until the Son of Man is
> raised from the dead.' [29]

Many people have been taught that this was an actual event in which Moses and Elijah emerged from Heaven (where many have been taught they are currently residing) and that they were physically present with the Messiah. These students often struggle with this biblical account because it appears that the Messiah was engaging in necromancy. Communication with the dead is a sin according

29. Matt. 17:1-9 ESV

to the Bible.[30] Was the Messiah sinning here? If He was, He is not qualified to be the Unblemished Lamb, and Moses and Elijah are conspirators in this abominable action with Him. This creates a doctrinal problem while trying to establish that Yeshua was, and is, indeed the Messiah.

There is a remedy to this problem, and it lies within the text itself, clearing up this confusion. In fact, terminology in "bookend" form is used here to provide more than sufficient clarity of what is occurring. Verse 3 reports that these figures "appeared" before them. The Greek word used is horao[31]. Moving down to verse 9 we read:

> And as they were coming down the mountain, Jesus commanded them, 'Tell no one the vision [haroma], until the Son of Man is raised from the dead.'

In some Bible versions, the word haroma is translated generically as "what you have seen" rather than the specific meaning this word carries throughout the Bible, which is "vision," such as is used in the text of the topic of this booklet. Few would suggest or interpret that an actual sheet of animals came out of the sky. It is understood that Peter's was a vision for a specific purpose, as is the case with Elijah and Moses "showing up" for Yeshua. The symbolism of the Law (Moses) and the Prophets (Elijah) "joining" with the Messiah is to present the agreement of these realities. That is the context of the transfiguration vision.

The vision symbolizes the Law and the Prophets are represented by these particular individuals speaking "with" Yeshua, so there is to be no doubt as to His Messianic status. Moses and Elijah were symbols of how the Law and the Prophets approved of, and were in agreement with, Yeshua. He brings all truth. This further solidifies the case that the Messiah did not

30. Lev 19:31; Lev 20:6; Lev 20:27; Deut 18:9-12; Isaiah 8:19

31. Strong's footnote 3708 horáō – properly, see, often with metaphorical meaning: "to see with the mind" (i.e. spiritually see), i.e. perceive (with inward spiritual perception)

bring with Him a new way, but that the ancient ways of Torah and prophetic truth in complete form were represented in unity with Him.

Animals were an excellent symbol for Peter's dream, for you can identify easily an animal as clean or unclean. People in the sheet would not be a good symbol because it would be difficult to identify from the appearance of a man if he is of faith. Nor would the action mechanism in the dream, "killing and eating," be appropriate with human symbols as that would be cannibalism. It works perfectly for animals to be the symbols, however, to convey acceptance of the clean animals for food violates no commandments. Moreover, even if the dream was about animals, though according to Peter it was not, did Adonai say that all animals were clean? No. He said that none were "common." There are no such things as common animals in the Torah.

If the vision was about all animals now being made clean, Peter would have gone out and taught this alteration of the dietary laws, but Peter was a disciple who had walked with Messiah and watched Him eat. If Peter had thought this vision meant this change, he would have taken this seriously and taught it outwardly. Rather, Peter, for the rest of his life, was a preacher of the gospel to those not born Jewish as well as to those from the Circumcision. There is no report of him teaching that the Torah dietary laws were changed or abolished, but his outreach to the nations is very well documented by biblical accounts.[32]

Moreover, if Peter's vision meant that no animals were to be considered unclean because of the Messiah, then how can we account for the "unclean" animals referenced in Revelation 18:2 in an event that has not occurred yet? What about Isaiah's prophecy for the future: "Those who sanctify and purify themselves to go into the gardens, following one in

32. Acts 9:32; 10:2

the midst, eating pig's flesh and the abomination and mice, shall come to an end together, declares the LORD."[33]

If Peter had gone out and eaten unclean animals or preached of a vision where Adonai instructed him to eat unclean, there would be significant historical documentation of this, as this would be an epic uproar of "biblical proportions." Many letters on this matter would ensue. None did. No one ever accused Peter of eating unclean or teaching anyone to eat unclean. Recall that some of the Sanhedrin were very against Yeshua, and they would have come down heavily on Peter as a disciple of Christ for teaching such things. The dietary laws had been in place for thousands of years, and Peter overturning this practice would be nothing short of societal chaos.

33. Isaiah 66:17
ESV

6

CONCLUSION

Peter's vision is not about the dietary laws. Bacon plays no part in this vision. It is an admonition by Adonai regarding Peter's wrong thinking that there were two separate groups of believers in God's eyes. Peter is told that there is only one nation under God, Israel, and once you are grafted in, you belong! Peter is told to get off the roof and go seek the sheep who were intermingled in the Gentile populations awaiting their summons and validation through the Messiah, Yeshua; they are indeed grafted into God's household, and they are invited to table fellowship just as if they had been born into it.

Peter was told graphically in a thrice-received vision that he was not to make distinctions between those who entered the covenant by birth into Israel and those who were not born into Israel, but they had taken hold the tzitzit of the Messiah:

> Thus says the LORD of hosts: In those days ten men from the nations of every tongue shall take hold of the robe of a Jew, saying, 'Let us go with you, for we have heard that God is with you.' [34]

34. Zechariah 8:23 ESV

This conclusion is consistent with the Torah. For the Word states:

> As for the assembly [church], there shall be one statute for you and for the alien who sojourns with you, a perpetual statute throughout your generations; You and the foreigner shall be the same before the Lord.[35]

This conclusion is also consistent with the purpose of Israel. Israel was to be a formed, collective example of His perfect government and community. Isaiah the prophet was very adamant about this: "I will appoint you as a covenant to the people, as a light to the nations." (42:6)

The Father's goal is to bring people out of their nations and into His nation. Israel was to obey the Torah as a beacon to lead people to Him, not to hide behind it. God's chosen messengers of the Word are to light the path to lead the sheep home, not to lead them to bacon! This vision is not about what kind of sandwich we can eat. It is about the inclusive role we have in the world to come. It's a beautiful message we can cling to with hope and confidence! Anyone grafted in through the Messiah is clean, even if they were not born of a tribe, and Israel is to go out and bring the sheep home! In Messiah, there is no such thing as "us and them."

35. Numbers 15:15 NASB

ONE Nation
ONE New Man
ONE Bride

The Body of Messiah is a Lighthouse with one dinner table...bacon-free.

QUESTIONS FOR REVIEW

1. What is the difference between "unclean" (*akatharton*) and "common" (*koinon*)?

2. What is the difference between "unlawful" (*anomia*) and "unlawful" (*athemitos*)?

3. The number 3 in scripture patterns symbolizes resurrection. Do you think there is a connection with the principle of resurrection considering that Peter had the vision 3 times? Why or why not?

4. What is the difference between "petras" and "petros"? How could not knowing the difference between these two words, or that both of these were used in the same sentence cause a misunderstanding in the text?

5. What does "bound" mean in regard to marital status?

6. What does "loosed" mean in regard to marital status?

7. Briefly, what is the oral law? What is the rabbinic law?

8. What is the *tallit gadol*?

9. What was the message Peter reports he was given through his vision?

10. Why was this vision so important in light of the commission Yeshua gave to Peter?

APPENDIX A

Brief Table of Clean and Unclean Animals

You shall therefore distinguish between clean animals and unclean, between unclean birds and clean, and you shall not make yourselves abominable by beast or by bird, or by any kind of living thing that creeps on the ground, which I have separated from you as unclean. And you shall be holy to Me, for I the LORD am holy, and have separated you from the peoples, that you should be Mine - Leviticus 20:25-26

(see next page for table)

CLEAN MEATS

LAND ANIMALS | Leviticus 11:3-8

Mammals that chew the cud and part the hoof

Antelope, Bison (bualo), Cattle (beef, veal), Caribou, Deer (venison), Elk, Gazelle, Girae, Goat, Hart, Ibex, Moose, Ox, Reindeer, Sheep (lamb, mutton)

WATER ANIMALS | Leviticus 11:9-12

Fish with fins and scales

Anchovy, Barracuda, Bass, Black pomfret (or monchong), Bluefish, Bluegill, Carp, Cod, Crappie, Drum, Flounder, Grouper, Grunt, Haddock, Hake, Halibut, Hardhead, Herring (or alewife), Kingfish, Mackerel (or corbia), Mahimahi (or dorado, dolphinfish [not to be confused with the mammal dolphin]), Minnow, Mullet, Perch (or bream), Pike (or pickerel or jack), Pollack (or pollock or boston bluefosh), Rockfish, Salmon, Sardine (or pilchard), Shad, Silver hake (or whiting), Smelt (or frost fish or ice fish), Snapper (or ebu, jobfish, lehi, onaga, opakapaka or uku), Sole, Steelhead, Sucker, Sunfish, Tarpon, Trout (or weakfish), Tuna (or ahi, aku, albacore, bonito, or tombo), Turbot (except european turbot), Whitefish

FLYING ANIMALS | Leviticus 11:13-19

Chicken, Dove, Duck, Goose, Grouse, Guinea fowl, Partridge, Peafowl, Pheasant, Pigeon, Prairie chicken, Ptarmigan, Quail, Sagehen, Sparrow (and other songbirds), Swan, Teal, Turkey

INSECTS | Leviticus 11:20-23

Insects with jointed, jumping legs

Types of locusts, including some crickets and grasshoppers

UNCLEAN MEATS

LAND ANIMALS | Leviticus 11:3-8

Land animals that do not chew the cud and part the hoof

CANINES: Coyote, Dog, Fox, Hyena, Jackal, Wolf
FELINES: Cat, Cheetah, Leopard, Lion, Panther, Tiger
EQUINES: Donkey, Horse, Mule, Onager, Zebra
SWINE: Boar, Peccary, Pig (bacon, ham, lard, pork)
OTHER: Armadillo, Badger, Bear, Beaver, Camel, Elephant, Gorilla, Groundhog, Hippopotamus, Kangaroo, Llama (alpaca, vicuña), Mole, Monkey, Mouse, Muskrat, Opossum, Porcupine, Rabbit (hare), Raccoon, Rat, Rhinoceros, Skunk, Slug, Snail (escargot), Squirrel, Wallaby, Weasel, Wolverine, Worm

WATER ANIMALS | Leviticus 11:9-12

Marine animals without fins and scales

FISH: Bullhead, Catfish, Eel, European Turbot, Marlin, Paddlefish, Shark, Stickleback, Squid, Sturgeon (includes most caviar), Swordfish
SHELLFISH: Abalone, Clam, Conch, Crab, Crayfish (crawfish, crawdad), Lobster, Mussel, Oyster, Scallop, Shrimp (prawn)
SOFT BODY: Cuttlesh, Jellysh, Limpet, Octopus, Squid (calamari)
SEA MAMMALS: Dolphin, Otter, Porpoise, Seal, Walrus, Whale

FLYING ANIMALS | Leviticus 11:13-19

Albatross, Bat, Bittern, Buzzard, Condor, Coot, Cormorant, Crane, Crow, Cuckoo, Eagle, Flamingo, Grebe, Grosbeak, Gull, Hawk, Heron, Kite, Lapwing, Loon, Magpie, Osprey, Ostrich, Owl, Parrot, Pelican, Penguin, Plover, Rail, Raven, Roadrunner, Sandpiper, Seagull, Stork, Swallow, Swift, Vulture, Water hen, Woodpecker

INSECTS | Leviticus 11:20-23

Insects without jointed, jumping legs

All insects except some in the locust family

REFERENCES

Catechism of the Catholic Church. "The Keys to the Kingdom #552." Retrieved November 1, 2016 from http://www.vatican. va/archive/ccc_css/archive/catechism/p122a3p3.htm.

Creeger, S. (2016). Introduction to the Jewish Sources: Preserving History, Structure, and Heart. Charleston, SC: BEKY Book Publications.

Foley, J. & Coffey, T., (Eds.) Sabbath Observance. (September 1, 1923. Vol. XLV) The Catholic Record. London, Canada. Retrieved November 1, 2016, from http://biblelight.net/c-record.htm

Ratzinger, C. J. (1994). Catechism of the Catholic Church. Liguori, MO: Liguori Publications, 36, 1954-1960.

ABOUT THE AUTHOR

Robin Gould, D.R.E., LMFT has a Master's Degree in Marriage & Family Therapy and a Doctorate in Religious Education. Practicing as a therapist since 2001, Dr. Gould specializes in Emotionally Focused Couple's Therapy and is currently conferencing on marital health, relationships, and attachment. She also travels as a lecturer and public speaker enlightening Christians to the Messiah in the Old Testament, as well as emphasizing the relational attachment aspects of the Torah to the Messianic  Believer. The proud mother of two wonderful sons, she divides her time between Florida and Vermont with her husband.

ACKNOWLEDGEMENTS

Thanks to Diane Schmid Laverty for her generous assistance in proofreading this booklet. She is a Godsend.

Thanks to Dr. Hollisa Alewine for her extensive contributions both in these pages as editor, and off these pages as an optimistic voice leading me to the paths of maturity and wisdom. Thank you for sharing your time and for investing in the community of women, helping their voices be heard for the Glory of the Kingdom. You are sincerely appreciated.

Thanks to my husband, David, for all of his love, encouragement, and motivation.

Thanks to Staci Bishop for being smart and on top of things.

81337554R00037

Made in the USA
Lexington, KY
19 February 2018